Hickey, The Days

HICKEY, THE DAYS
ARE WIDER THAN THE SKY

Poems by J.H. BEALL

Published by
THE WORD WORKS, INC. P.O. Box 4054, Washington, D.C. 20015
1980

First Edition
Printed 1980
Printed USA

No part of this book may be
reproduced without the express
permission of the publisher.

Copyright, © James Beall, 1980
Library of Congress Card Number: 0-015380-09-9
International Standard Book Number: 79-65-655

The WORD WORKS, Inc. gratefully
acknowledges the grant from the D.C. Commission
on the Arts and Humanities, the support of our
contributors, and the services donated by many
talented individuals, which made this publication
possible.

Contents

Part I

13 Ghost Prints
14 For Tara
16 What The Astronaut Considers The Evening Before A Flight
17 The Quiet Sun
18 Taurus X-I
19 Wireless
20 A Black Stick
21 March 7, 1970
22 The First Poetic Tribute To Lon Chaney In The History of English Lit.
23 Varicosity
26 Snow Angels
27 Blue Shift

Part II

31 Easter
32 King Kong Vs. Godzilla
33 Monologue Of The Rabbit
34 Careful Conversations
35 Motorcycle Ride At Midnight
36 A Night In The Country
37 Spiderwork
38 The Hitchhiker's Thanksgiving
39 Rectilinear Motion In An Azimuthally Symmetric Universe
40 Abscission Layer
41 In Praise Of Outrageous Women
42 A Christmas Present for Grammarians
43 Hickey, The Days
45 Christmas Returns:

Part III

49 A Winter Song
50 Machines Of Weather
51 The Slow Curve Of Forget-Me-Nots
52 Indiana State Highway Patrol
53 Spectator Sports
54 For Hart Crane
55 The Bathtub Drain Poem
56 Apartment Living
57 Night Train From The City
58 Afterimage
59 A Grammatical Construction Of The Sacred

Part IV

63 Nero
64 Onions
66 Sandcastles
67 Corinth

Acknowledgements

Some of the poems have appeared in the following publications: "Calvert Review," "The Hollins Critic," "Three Sisters," "The Pacifica Paper," and "Pod" (London), and in the following anthologies: *City Celebration* and *The Poet Upstairs*.

This book was typeset by Sue Hoth and printed by Paul Trimble at The Writer's Center Bookworks (Glen Echo, Maryland), which is partially funded by grants from the National Endowment for the Arts, The Maryland Arts Council, and the Kiplinger Foundation. Design Consultant: Kevin Osborn

for Judson and Lenore Beall, and for Tara

Ghost Prints

      Nothing vanishes.
      As the kettle steams
the water disappears
      yet
           on the windows
           interleaved between
the cold outside
      and the vapors
the condensation
      outlines
      the handprint
           that you made
           where you leaned too far
      to see the sky.

For Tara

Standing on flowers, lashes and rainbows
in a dead sky, smiling. Happy face.
Standing in stations,
    trains waiting as the cold
    comes rumbling in.
    Reaching to hug me
    heart in my heartening
    kiss and the wide eyes
    surprise.
When you go
I will be a snowflake
melting.

The Quiet Sun

It burns its years into us,
softly.
Beneath it, the mountains sleep
their blue dreams.

Tomorrow starts at midnight,
the highest hour.
If we find meadows there,
let them be grazed clean
by light.

What The Astronaut Considers The Evening Before A Flight

     Well, now. She is a beautiful
woman and you are an astronaut, and
tomorrow when the engines light
they may light the wrong way

     or the hairline crack or weakness
in the steel the inspector yawned over
may blossom in the guts
of the combustion chamber and death

     will blossom for you, an orange flower,
and you will fall instead of being
driven up like the other times,
a fist like god's shoving, accelerating

     you up and up into the careless blue
of less and less air fading into purple,
the deepest darkness and stars. Rocketry
is not as careless as it seems.

     She is quite beautiful. She is
naked, sleeping on your bed, your semen in her
doing whatever it does afterward,
the sperm wiggling up, looking

     for a ripe egg. You are careful,
though. You have made love once already
and you think you should maybe do it
again because it's going to be a long

     flight, nights waking from the dream
about falling, awake and falling still,
always falling. You pull yourself out
of the cover that holds you, floating

to get the book, and read. Your light
casts its warm cone on the page before you.
You touch your hand to the cold window.
You think you feel the heat from tiny stars

    imbedded in black glass. She is sleeping.
The night bugs make their tinny sounds
so much like the hiss in the radio when no one
transmits. It is the whisper of stars.

    She floats through this sound, sleep
is her ship that rockets her sometimes, now
turning, now a frown, now silent. Floating
now or perhaps dreaming of the fall.

    The cat makes its happy mutterings lap
about her ears. She hears the ocean.
She is a sailor now. She is in you as much
as you are in her. Years have done this.

    The tracks intertwined. The times
you sleep together all there, tugging.
The kindness and the anger. You distort
each other's worlds. This gravity makes

    your orbits very close. You dance now.
One swings the other, pushes, thrusts
or pulls, coming, coming very close.
These movements form eccentric orbits

    of the heart. What more can one
say? She is warm and beautiful
and her mass draws you nearer.
In the distance, through the dark,

    still an extension of the earth's
dark meanings, the rocket
begins to take on fuel.

Taurus X-1
for George Pennington

    Like light, the years
break into their rainbow colors
and we measure their passing
as we measure the winking out
of stars: first, the brilliance
we look to; then, nothing.
Even the nothing is too late,
by the minutes or years that measure
the distance between us.

    I was living on another planet.
My life ran parallel to yours,
but differently. The sky is a different
color here. I think of you often.

    That constellation is Taurus.
Astrologers say it is my own. In it,
the Crab Nebula is seed spread out
into the sky, the remnant of a star.
We watch these things a thousand years
too late, but we watch them.

    When the cancer began walking
within the nebulosity of your lungs,
your lungs broke into filaments
from the shock. Shortly,
there was nothing.

    Your pieces have returned
to their dark ground. We are
the remnants of your passing.

Wireless

Air rubbing
air around a corner's hard to tell
    from distant talk. I look up
    like a dog
    disturbed in sleep, muttering a bark,
    opening my eyes in time
        to see my syllables
        unleashed into the wind
        floating free.

A Black Stick

It is not exactly as snow, this falling.
Their science does not enamor me.
I have lived too long in its shadow.
    The bag of oranges on the table
is lit by the grey, sleet-storm light.
    The impossible spheres defy weather.
    They are brought in leaden crates
    that dragons carry on their backs.

When I turn the switch, do I stir
demons who think of light?
My pencil's trail is graphite
    and plastic. It could be
    a snake frozen by my will.

In view of this, what is our hold
on the world? In this desert, we
have grasped (so carelessly)
    a black stick, straight and strong,
    to walk with.

    Now it comes alive
    in our hands.

March 7, 1970

At noon notice how
in the eclipse
the heat goes. Since it's March,
    the winter circles
      closer in.

    In the darkened room
we pin-hole the image to the floor
and make love while the sun
winks on your tit.

**The First Poetic Tribute To Lon Chaney
In the History of English Lit.**

Lovers in the full moon.
Not werewolves, but
    you will take my silver bullet
    moaning low, lie down shedding
    layers of clothes
    and Lon Chaney faces
    till all traces drop
    to death and spent spells.

Varicosity

I
The sunset behind the old couple lights
cumulus towers orange and red to the east.
One nearer cloud remains white and casts
its light upon the river's darker dark.

They stand on the dock. He fishes.
She just looks to where the schools of minnows
leap in unison and break the light surface
into concentric nights. Fish jump everywhere,

even in the river's reflection
of the watered air, and on
the woman's white legs
the red and blue veins like a school
of minnows all leaping together
breaking the white surface.

II
Here the river runs wide and slow,
licking the land with its salt tongues.
Nothing of the land here does not give
itself to the river where it can.

The rest, too high, waits for weather.
At noon, from the shore, he sees
the white shark's teeth of sailboats
drawing themselves along back and forth
mocking the wind.

III
The shells are locked in these rocks
that are eaten and decayed by water
coming, leaving. The fossil mollusks
that had once burrowed in some homely mud

have been thrown up by the river,
by the rivers of dark stone that move
and yield. Finally, the brittle pieces
wash out smaller and finer. She picks up

this one in her hands and twists
to see at what point the layers remaining
will fail and fall back.

IV
To settle or unsettle this mountain's
accounts with itself must have taken
years, here where the road cuts through
letting the strata show and leap.

Plunging past these layers,
they talk some. The weather.
The intermittent whittling of the wind
at the car's side vents adds itself

to some dim rush of wonder that goes
by them without comment. They travel
the clear sweep where the road
cuts through, topping the long rise

into purple dark and red rocks,
then out again into open air and blueness
until the road arcs down to farms
and the other mountains.

V
What hurtles on its way is not
the brittle air that passes, or the journey,
but some fluid that breaks around them
as they move. As someone walking by

the night river might take a step and find
his feet wreathed in the blue fluorescence
of microscopic life, so they, moving further,
notice that legs and belly, the strands of hair,

even the teeth glow. They are naked now.
They trail a cool, blue fire. The wind
that ripples the water's surface
speckles their reflections with light.

Snow Angels

There is no sufferance here.
How the old line of hills fades
into the winter sky
is still a mystery. What began
essential still is.

I made snow angels, letting
the gray flakes fall
from the light sky onto me
as I flapped and struggled.
When I arose, the snow showed
nothing of me. Showed only
the imprint of the twisting creature
that I still look for.

Snow fell all day
and covered it, only outlines left.
Winter wore on
in successive thaws and freezes.
Grass grew, eventually,
into my memory of it.

It wings its way back
now and then. I like
the returning of it,
though I no longer
believe in angels.

Blue Shift

In this age
there is no limit but light
our eyes can stand
    the incredible blue rushes toward us
    our centers reel
    from the shocks we make.

Looking backward, the past scenes
tinge to red. The fallen photographs
begin to yellow now
    one last look back, taking
    what we can remember.

Even the lightest load becomes massive.
The very thoughts seem to carry
great weight. Yet here
    in this small beginning
    the things we carry do not
    make us slow
    as they might seem to.

We move like ions in the night
of ghostly stars
a faint path left to track us
    while the world condenses
    in a ring
    at the periphery
    like dew.

Part II

Easter

The morning casts its blue light
like dice in forgotten alleys.
The trees hold blueness in their
green air. Somewhere, children
in their lairs can dream
of chocolate rabbits.

Here, the world is real. Light becomes
lavender. The tired faces of the people
here will not sing hymns or shine,
though they might, later, wish to.
The sky bleeds pink into cold night.

In the work oblivion wends them
into, the sweating cook, the dazed
waitress, customers in a stupor
of sleep or booze
keep their single appointment
with the day. The red ball of the sun
rises over Jerusalem.

King Kong Vs. Godzilla

The Washington monument
is a mechanical monster
that was left on the mall
by a bankrupt science fiction
    movie crew
        too poor even
            to disassemble the thing
            or disconnect the batteries.
At night, its eight, beading,
red eyes (two on a side)
ward off airplanes.

Someday,
bored of being tickled
by the sightseers within,
    it will rear up
    on its great, hidden legs
    (conveniently buried under the mall)
    and march on New York
        to beat the hell out of
        the Empire State Building,
        its only worthwhile rival.

Monologue Of The Rabbit

Where we came from
    there are no restrictions.

I am a rabbit in his den
dug up by hounds
my ribcage
    rattles me under the fence
    the sharp wire
    to safety.
My lungs
sting
at the wet air.

The dogs get through
    only slowly.
My scent is left
    they are coming
      but more distant now.

    There is no pattern to the world
    only its flight.

Careful Conversations

    With Abbott and Costello glances,
furtive at each other's friendliness
(and chances), we meet again, long days away,
still lovers.

    Yet we know so many things, it seems
a shame to waste the time on subtle, careful
conversations, while the sheets are waiting,
fresh and pink and clean.

Motorcycle Ride At Midnight
for Tom Horne

My vision yellows in the faceplate, turning
the moon and clouds the color of old milk.
    The patient, numbing fingers of the wind
begin their stitching, needles working in.
    We wed the thread of cold air to our bones.

The road we ride on, in this frictioned night
pitched over the rolling land before us
    through the halt and distant convergence
of the trees, sings to us in the tires.
    And though the round gauges float

and feather as an afterimage of the night
the cars burn holes in, we go on
    and on. You touch the button of the horn.
A frail sound, a thin eggshell of air
    expands into the wind.

A Night In The Country

The gray clouds, like the undersides
of geese in winter, incubating
for days and days, have hatched the moon,
pecking through.

The wind is drying white feathers
from the goldenrods. In fields, the darkness
stirs. There are things in the air,
like bats, navigating on their own sound,

and the trees are night's lovers, listening
while the wind pulls their hair out.

Spiderwork

In the gentle time, working his silver threads,
sutures up the warm blood,
the dry rustle of insects. Before that,
certainly, was despair.

    In the gentle time, working his sutures up,
closing the skin in
        breath
            air.
What must this green room be like?
    The careful anesthesias, then
    translucent, he enters, singing.
    Certainly, some sense of this
    impending,
    before those needles, before
    that old razor.

The Hitchhiker's Thanksgiving

    The road is as bare as the trees
of this winter, and the silence sings
    along the highway like tires.
It keeps a harmony with the wind.

    I stick my thumb up, sampling
the watered light, the chill, the wary glances
    from the lone cars going by me.
Humming to themselves, they must think
    of turkey, the log fires.

This road, step by step,
is eating me for dinner.

Rectilinear Motion In An Azimuthally Symmetric Universe

    I am watching the evening go helpless,
the earth rolling and the down sliding sky
    like the color complement of a Pepto-Bismol
commercial.
    Night wells into its sweet womb
    and the flubug is foiled
    by the icky-iced stars
    and the sugar coated plum of Jupiter
    in total noon.

I am so ill I may vomit the world up.

Abscission Layer
>   *To Martha Swain Edwards*

     I stand at window watching night and wind
as one in wrestling leaves across the yard.
     The tree branch semaphoring streetlamp chides
my hope of summer with its barren guard.

     The footsteps in the dark have drawn me here
perched by the window, hopeful of some prey.
     A coughing voice denies the empty street
where no one hurries, evening has its way.

     The world is shuttered tight, but now and then
some distant voices echo in the lulls
     of rattling leaves. Below me nothing but
the waste of autumn, wind-whipped to the walls.

In Praise Of Outrageous Women

All the women I know are outrageous.
I seem to attract them. They are like
flies going to their destiny.
This one wields her words like meat axes,
so carefully controlled they can split hairs
I didn't even see. Others, in the tradition
of the old west, forget to take their spurs
off at night. This habit leaves its mark.

All the women I know are outrageous.
They ask me to take them to parties,
or I ask to take them to parties
and they go. Once we arrive, I do not
see them 'till it's time to leave. I do not
complain about this because I know
they have broken at least three hearts
in their absence from me. I consider myself
spared.

All the women I know are outrageous,
and when the sadness strikes them
like thunder peeling the sky open
or the copper blur and gaping pink mouth
of the viper, they grip my arm or hand
very tight. We are stopped, then,
by the street musician's music that weaves
itself around us like a spell.

All the women I know are outrageous.
They will dance and dance to this music
until the sadness is shucked from around them
like a cocoon.

A Christmas Present For Grammarians

    How shall I say this?
For a metaphor, I give you land . . .
    Which means:
        the moon and stars, the trees,
        the windward ocean, and since giving
        is the season
        its dichotomy as well, the city.
In it:
        men and ships and reason,
        the field of numbers and the garden
        of talk.

We walk and touch
and in our varied worlds combine the two —
the only animal yet known
              who do!

Hickey, The Days

    Hickey, the days are wider than the sky
and this weather that the snow makes up
    like stories of some after-Christmas night
when the songs lull themselves to sleep
    is filled with smoke and blue winter
warm on the unused buttons of my coat.

    The quiet sleeps in my ears and the wind
rustles the city, its many faces, like leaves,
    only for an instant. Then the sound returns
by way of a distant cab horn that echoes,
    starts the avalanche of soft sound falling
on my ears like snow.

    Hickey, if I would I could tell you
what the weather is where it leads and burns
    my skin, and I go on like this for hours like leaves
my dry skin with your sweet touch. I sleep.
    This is far away to tell an echo of mountains
from the plains and tell the flatness, toll it out
    like bells.

    I would want you knowing how the weather goes
the shift of seasons as they come and curl
    around us that begins begins begins
I try to feel. I could ask all else
    would not you give me night, a cup of it,
so warm and black that I can drink and feel
    the burning as the center goes?

    Hickey, I have tried some magic on you,
when the sky fills up with grayness, tombstones,
    and they march on happiness the fort. Indians
would. I stamp the dust, then mud. Get mostly wet.
    For all this, I have lost nothing, shades,
horizons, my front yard. White winter later
    and bare trees, your face in puddles the rain
    ripples.

    Sets it all to mind, my giving up.
    I love you well enough and will not.

Christmas Returns:

    the long lines of winter
    taking the presents back
    smoke and condensation
of the brittle voices catching in the air.
    the slush streets as snow leaves us
    cold water in the mornings
for our faces since the heater broke.

    I pocket years like hands
    avoid the chill.

A Winter Song

Grey days in Pittsburgh,
steel city full of rain
and cold.
    The winter hold of bus rides,
    thirty-five cent fares,
    apartments where
    warm chairs waited, tired and glad,
    that anybody's footsteps had
    awakened them to see
    that she was looking
    as I sat and smiled.
    How she beguiled the winter,
    letting down her hair.

Machines of Weather

The umbrella is
    a black crow hanging
    in my shower.

I brought him in from weather,
from the grey sky,
plucked him
in a field of flowers
with cumuliform heads.
    He rustles,
    drips his ideas to the drain.

The Slow Curve Of Forget-Me-Nots

In the laboratory, the pigeons
are drumming
    (rain on a cardboard box)
The pilot bulbs form
dim instruments
    out of darkness.
    Needles quiver, moved by
    ghosts of air
    but the reinforcement stopped.

The pigeons, pecking, slow
and ponder
(or only slow)
    pecking.
This frequency-over-time
their own velocity
is dropping down
in the slow curve of forget-me-nots
of food.
    Flowers
    I
    remember
    well enough.

Indiana State Highway Patrol

Even as I rest, the road runs through me
white concrete
sharpened by the distance
to a fine point where it sticks
into the horizon like the thorn
that left itself in my skin
to swell and fester.

There are times when
the black asphalt back roads
hiss with my tires as the black snake
sliding through that one early morning
up the tree. I blow his skin off
with my shotgun. His pink meat
drops like ripe fruit.

Here, my wife sleeps beside me.
Her white breasts curve
in a cold vision of winter.

Spectator Sports

    I am watching the men play flootball,
touch and tackle on the sloping ground,
ball falling   wobble bouncing crazy
on uneven turf.
    I am watching the men play football.
Three figures taking keep-away turns at
throwing laughs and moans. Mistakes
come to me split seconds late under
the grey, sweatshirt sky.

    They are pausing, talking strategy,
changing plans. Limp wrists dangle
from the weight of seconds. Football's
under arm, pigskin closeup, smelling the cold
and armhair stinks, almost squealing
with delight and the numb fingers wrapped
around its dumb disguise of leather,
ready to be tossed up
    into alien skies.

For Hart Crane

Sun in the winter
the Mexico mountain air
    and your heart-shaped
    sailor tattoo
    mother on his arm
    as you approached
    he popped the candy
    to his mouth you
    salivate and
        his sneering
        causes you to jump
you thrown by
    the wave that curls his lip
    over the back breakers
    of the ship's last wake
        then silence   then the sharks
          the candy wrapper floating
            on fluorescent seas.

The Bathtub Drain Poem

My bathtub drain is stopped up.
The hairs you left, your long trademarks,
have worked their way down
to the unsuspecting bend in the pipes
and lodged there, waiting for Draino
or eternity.

I am sweating over the plunger
like some laborer, pulling to deliver
the wad of hair from the iron pipe
into the white world. I am as useless
to you as the wind is, moving,
yet failing to move, the roots of you.
The idea of it sticks in my throat.

Apartment Living

    If the sounds weren't familiar,
they would cut through the walls.
    Her ululations come. His dark curses
come. The sounds skip in and out, through
    some "F-Layer" of noise, due to some
acoustic sunspot cycle, or (perhaps)
    the inconsistency of rage.

    I cage the room with paces, fret
the phonebook with my fingers, dial
    and undial the phone, and finally
call the police.

    I see my neighbors in the morning
leave for work. I say hello.

Night Train From The City

The train lows across the surface of the land,
the strong, steel tracks. Within, the riders
pitch and roll, pitch and roll. The back alleys,
the outer faces, fade from the window, wane

to cabin lights, reflections of the legs
across the aisle. By itself, the train contains
nothing. Even its power comes along thin wires
hanging overhead, comes on demand of the motors,

the men controlling. The people in this motion,
this unconstrained, this headlong flight, pushed
by the distant stations, pulled by the distant towns,
along the lowing rails, cold and bright, must be

tethered as the steel in the heart
of these machines. There, each string
tuned to shadows, tuned to night,
strikes up its song, and sings.

Afterimage

This sadness stains me
as iodine stains my skin
deep purple, or, if I rub it
quick enough, most swirling down
the coriolis of the sink
like purple clouds,
then yellow, stains me yellow,
a faint residue on my skin
indistinguishable
from an old bruise.

I would have looked longer
if I could. The red sun, quilted
through black trees, hung there
for an instant. As I look away
the disc remains
floats before me, changing colors
growing smaller with the night.

When I have touched you
the memory holds my skin
for hours. The smells
that have worked themselves
into pores, come out slowly,
launch themselves into air
that surrounds me, that
touches as I turn,
asks the dim brain
to bring you there.

I pass other women.
The afterimage of your face
blinks on their faces
like the sun.

A Grammatical Construction Of The Sacred

The sky is pink and lavender
in the dusk. I am coming down
from the hills, and I still do not
understand. A slow cross shadows

its dark movement through
the sky. Its belly, in this half light,
seems open. Conjecture of its content
rambles in my head, a gale of words

below the dimmest words,
the sound of its engine.
Nothing is the same for me.
The usual faces in the clouds
have changed. I impress myself,
remember her name, my convictions.
These were my people, and though
they have quarreled with me, some

firm beginning led me to believe
I could change and meet them, also changed.
    I have traveled in unorthodox fashion.
    My blood steamed once in the cutting air.
    They have moved themselves in my absence.
    I have outgrown.

Nero

In the bears' and wolves' clothing they come
with bared knives through the streets
that are blood's rivers, and we are helpless,
our armies and temples ruin. There is only one prayer,
now:

    If we are to be known, let
    our last act be music
    drawn from this bow and string,
    tapped from the keg of the air's
    latency, drawn fine and resinous,
    harboring the old, fallen rituals.

Let the music spin from our
civilization webs like light
that will spread the ghost of these
dry centuries into space, so that
those moving here in the silence
that will surely follow
will feel the faint brush of these days
across their arms and faces.

Onions

      In the end, we lose everything,
even the center,
         peeling the layers down.
         The small mouse nibbles
         at my heart. His teeth are sharp
         and cause a quiet pain here
         inside, where there is no echo.
         It is so close and warm.

      In the mountains, it is raining.
      The small town sleeps
      in its robe of lights. The darkness
      is so gentle it will not
      be kept at bay.
When the air is warm, even darkness,
we do not think. The inside
         of the brain is so much light. Yet
         it must be dark in there, behind
         the eyes.

      Her skin, I thought, would
      be suffused in a pale blue
light as we lay together there,
darkness for a blanket,
         but it was only love, and I
         confused the center, her for
         the vast systems of the sun.

    The earth turns, first green,
then digging deeper, spade
the darkness out, and the worms'
wriggling, pale flesh.
    The red thread through the center
    (almost like the string in a bandaid)
    is blood.

    The earth turns and drags
the daylight out like a thin,
white paste. I know
the feeling when it dries
must come to tingles,
the electric sensations
nestling in, diving to darkness,
back to the original
interpretation, away
from the skull's quick,
supposed light.

Sandcastles

At dusk, we pack wet sand
into the hollows of blue air
to make our battlements.

The towers take on life
of their own when we squat
to see them against the last light.

It is morning, now. We walk past
the single, dessicated remnant,
ruined by the sun.

Corinth

I. The layers of earth contain
themselves and the patterns
that we fit from finding
as the pick rings in the dry earth.
Here the walls crumbled in
to seal the breaking pots. Yet
these sad fingers, sweeping
the years away with their careful
movements, to which century
do they belong?

II. The sun rests in its high flight
on crystal pillars of air. The dust
holds even the dark eyes' watching.
Only the radio bothers to speak.
There is no freedom in the weather.

III. One day, the people danced and laughed
and painted the town back into
the old names. They talked politics
then, beneath the black no-names
of shadows and the new smears of paint.
Everywhere, the light washed their world
clean as though nothing had happened.

IV. They lay together the first night,
his olive cock parting her
blond hair and her lips. With the dawn,
she sank back into the present,
stumbling up the road.
A whore called her name and she
did not answer. Her lover's
spit sank into the earth.

V. So much to the present. So much
to the past. The air holds
the ghost of these cities shimmering
in hot fists. When he opens
his hand to clutch her, even
the mirage disappears. He cannot
remember the words she taught
in that strange language while
the sky swam white with the gauze
of stars so like her skin. He
thought of how the darkness parted
the Milky Way like he had parted
her, and wondered what it meant.

VI. She left the ruins and the village
and only thought of the differences.
His night became her day. She watched
the same sky with no
particular conviction.

VII. They discussed the lovers,
those that remained, over evenings
on the cafe terrace, but talked
in English. The boy, passing,
heard some distant word he thought
had happened before, but could not
remember.

VIII. "Sometimes (the words came from
an old woman) the path
changes slowly, with many feet."

IX. In the shed, the remnants,
pots, shards, slivers, faded
and curved into recognition,
lay sensually with one another,
consistently old. One silver
tool is left from her
working. It changes the forms of the forest
of broken earth
by its presence. There,
in the drawer, no one notices
the changing
for a long time.

X. Afterwards, the sun
mounts to its same position
in the sky. The earth
receives its heat again,
but the light is older.
The air beneath moves
in freedom its liquid hips.

Photo: Kathleen Wright

Jim Beall was born and raised on a farm in central West Virginia. He has received a B.A., an M.S., and a Ph.D. in physics, and is currently a Congressional Fellow for the U.S. Congress Office of Technology Assessment. His interests are wide-ranging and include astrophysics and public policy. His daughter, Tara, was born in 1970. An early manuscript of this book was a finalist in the 1977 Houghton Mifflin New Poets Series.